Follow Me Around™
South Korea

By Wiley Blevins

SCHOLASTIC

Content Consultant: Dafna Zur, PhD, Assistant Professor of East Asian Languages and Cultures
Stanford University, Stanford, California

Library of Congress Cataloging-in-Publication Data
Names: Blevins, Wiley, author.
Title: South Korea / by Wiley Blevins.
Description: New York, NY : Children's Press, 2018. | Series: Follow me around | Includes bibliographical references and index.
Identifiers: LCCN 2017057942 | ISBN 9780531129227 (library binding) | ISBN 9780531138649 (pbk.)
Subjects: LCSH: Korea (South)—Juvenile literature. | Korea
(South)—Description and travel—Juvenile literature.
Classification: LCC DS902 .B64 2018 | DDC 951.95—dc23
LC record available at https://lccn.loc.gov/2017057942

Design: Anna Tunick Tabatchnick
Creative Direction: Judith E. Christ for Scholastic Inc.
Text: Wiley Blevins
© 2019 Scholastic Inc.

1 2 3 4 5 6 7 8 9 10 R 28 27 26 25 24 23 22 21 20 19

Photos ©: cover background: Guitar Photographer/Shutterstock; cover children: Topic Images/Getty Images; back cover: Topic Images/Getty Images; 1: Topic Images/Getty Images; 3: PortForLio/HD Signature Co., Ltd/Alamy Images; 4 background: jkjk0342/Multi-bits/ImaZinS/Getty Images; 4 children: Topic Images/Getty Images; 6: Jung Yeon-Je/AFP/Getty Images; 7 left: SeongJoon Cho/Bloomberg/Getty Images; 7 right: Albert Tan photo/Moment/Getty Images; 8 left: Caro/Sorge/Newscom; 8 center left: 4kodiak/iStockphoto; 8 center right: whitewish/iStockphoto; 8 center: F.G.I./age fotostock; 9 top: MiXA/Getty Images; 9 bottom: Y_L/Shutterstock; 10: Topic Images/Getty Images; 11: Pascal Deloche/Photononstop/Getty Images; 11: Sidhe/Shutterstock; 12 left: IMAGEMORE/Alamy Images; 12 right: Daria Ustiugova/Shutterstock; 12-13 background: Vadim Yerofeyev/Dreamstime; 13 left: Seok Nanhee/TongRo Images/Alamy Images; 13 right: Holly Looney/Imagemore/Superstock, Inc.; 14 top left: suntill/Multi-bits/ImaZinS/Getty Images; 14 bottom: fotoVoyager/iStockphoto; 14 top right: Manfred Gottschalk/Lonely Planet Images/Getty Images; 15 top left: John W Banagan/Lonely Planet Images/Getty Images; 15 bottom: Robert Koehler/Moment/Getty Images; 15 top right: Byeongsu Guk/EyeEm/Getty Images; 16 top left: Philippe Turpin/Photononstop/Superstock, Inc.; 16 top center: Jaewon Lee/Alamy Images; 16 top right: Jaewon Lee/Alamy Images; 16 bottom: PortForLio/HD Signature Co., Ltd/Alamy Images; 17 top left: jeryltan/iStockphoto; 17 bottom: hanoded/iStockphoto; 17 top right: Henn Photography/Cultura/Getty Images; 18 left: Iberfoto/The Image Works; 18 right: DEA/G. Dagli orti/The Granger Collection; 19 left: Pictures from History/The Granger Collection; 19 center: World History Archive/Superstock, Inc.; 19 right: RIA Novosti/The Image Works; 20 top left: RUNSTUDIO/DigitalVision/Getty Images; 20 top right: tgladkova/Shutterstock; 20 bottom: Noam Galai/Getty Images; 21 top: Im Yeongsik/iStockphoto; 21 bottom left: IMAGEMORE/age fotostock; 21 bottom right: David Sanger/The Image Bank/Getty Images; 22 left: Sagase48/Shutterstock; 22 right: PortForLio/HD Signature Co., Ltd/Alamy Images; 23 top: Chung Sung-Jun/Getty Images; 23 center top: Jung Yeon-Je/AFP/Getty Images; 23 center bottom: Jeonghyeon Noh/Dreamstime; 23 bottom: Yonhap News/YNA/Newscom; 24 center: Fiona Hanson/PA Images/Getty Images; 24 left: Menno Boermans/Aurora Photos; 24 right: PortForLio/HD Signature Co., Ltd/Alamy Images; 25 left: Saran_Poroong/Shutterstock; 25 right: JTB Photo/age fotostock; 26 top left: Insung Jeon/Moment/Getty Images; 26 top right: Zerbor/iStockphoto; 26 bottom left: Tzido/iStockphoto; 26 bottom right: Lee Jin-man/AP Images; 27 bottom left: cyoginan/iStockphoto; 27 top left: Koldunov/iStockphoto; 27 top right: Jimin&Hyerim/TongRo Images/Alamy Images; 28 A.: meunierd/Shutterstock; 28 B.: Nghia Khanh/Shutterstock; 28 C.: Topic Images/Getty Images; 28 D.: ARTYOORAN/Shutterstock; 28 G.: Nghia Khanh/Shutterstock; 28 F.: Sung-woo Cho/Dreamstime; 28 E.: Dmitry Chulov/Shutterstock; 30 top right: flowgraph/iStockphoto; 30 top left: Leontura/iStockphoto; 30 bottom: Topic Images/Getty Images.

Maps by Jim McMahon/Mapman ®.

Front cover: Fireworks in Incheon

Table of Contents

Where in the World Is South Korea?

Annyŏng haseyo (ahn-yong ha-seh-yoh) from South Korea! That's how we say "hello." My name is Wook-jin. I'll be your tour guide, along with my little sister Yu-na. We welcome you to our beautiful country.

South Korea is in Asia. It is located on the Korean **Peninsula**. Our country also includes more than 3,000 islands. Two of them have volcanoes. There are many fun and interesting places to see. Let's get going!

4

Fast Facts:

- South Korea covers 38,502 square miles (99,720 square kilometers).

- South Korea is surrounded by three bodies of water: the Yellow Sea, East Sea (other countries call it the Sea of Japan), and West Sea (or East China Sea).

- North Korea lies to the north.

- Mountains cover 70 percent of the country. The Sobaek Mountains are in the south. The Taebaek Mountains are in the north.

- South Korea's longest river is the Nakdong River. It is 325 miles (523 km) long.

- Jeju Island is the largest island in South Korea. It is more than twice the size of New York City, but with a fraction of the population.

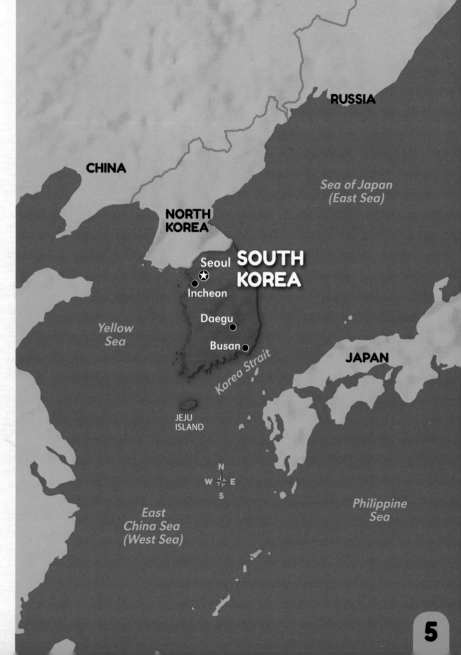

RUSSIA

CHINA

Sea of Japan
(East Sea)

NORTH
KOREA

Seoul **SOUTH
KOREA**

Incheon

Yellow
Sea

Daegu

Busan

JAPAN

Korea Strait

JEJU
ISLAND

N
W E
S

East
China
Sea
(West Sea)

Philippine
Sea

Last Names

Our family name is Kim. In South Korea, we say our family name first. So, my official name is Kim Wook-jin. My sister's is Kim Yu-na. It's like you saying "Smith Jack" instead of "Jack Smith." But you can call us Wook-jin and Yu-na.

About 20 percent of South Koreans have the last name Kim. About half of all Koreans have one of these last names: Kim, Lee, Choi, and Pak (also spelled Park).

Home Sweet Home

We are from Seoul, the country's capital. My sister and I live in a big apartment building with our *emoni* (uh-muh-nee, mother) and *aboji* (ah-buh-jee, father). Our parents work for high-tech companies. They bring home lots of fun tech gadgets for my sister and me to play with and use.

If you visit our home, I recommend wearing clean socks. And make sure they have no holes! We take off our shoes before entering our home.

Verandas

Clay and wood house

Our apartment has front and back verandas. A veranda is a type of porch. Our family often sits on the front veranda. The back veranda is off the kitchen. We use it for storing items and washing clothes.

Many South Korean homes are heated by a system located under their floors. It's called an *ondol* (on-dohl). Ondols have been used for 3,000 years! Our family sleeps on mats on the floor, and the ondol keeps us warm. Some of our friends, however, have beds in bed frames with legs, like many kids in other countries have.

Older homes are made of clay and wood. Our grandparents live in one of these homes. My little sister prefers their home to our apartment.

Being Polite

Manners are very important here. It is common to give gifts to friends. We also bow to those older than we are. And losing your temper is a big no-no!

Kimchi

Bi bim bap

Beef soup

Let's Eat!

When it comes to food, we like spicy! Red pepper, green onion, soy sauce, bean paste, garlic, ginger, sesame, and mustard are favorites. Every meal includes white rice and a pickled vegetable called *kimchi* (kihm-chee). Kimchi is our national dish. There are more than 100 different kinds. It might be made from cabbage, cucumbers, or radishes.

Our family eats together at a low table. For breakfast many days, my sister and I eat bean sprout soup and white rice with steamed vegetables. For lunch, *bi bim bap* (bee bihm bahp) is a favorite. It is a bowl of rice covered with vegetables and served with an egg. We also eat juicy watermelon. For dinner, our mom likes to make simple dishes such as beef and radish soup.

At the Table

- The oldest person is the first to start eating.
- Never use your fingers to tear food.
- Do not leave your chopsticks in your rice bowl.
- Don't blow your nose at the table.
- Everyone stays until the oldest person is finished.

If you ever visit, try *pulgogi* (pul-goh-gee), Korean barbecue. It's popular all over the world. Meat is cooked at the table on a hot plate or small grill. We also love *kimbap* (kihm-bahp), or seaweed rolls. Our mom makes them for picnics.

To end the meal, you should have *yakgwa* (yahk-gwah). It's a fried cookie made with honey, ginger, sesame oil, and pine nuts. My sister can't stop eating them! My favorite treat is *songpyeon* (song-pyung). That's rice cakes shaped like half-moons and stuffed with sweet seeds, nuts, or a tasty paste.

Forget about forks and knives when eating in South Korea. We use spoons to eat soup and rice. We eat everything else with chopsticks. You'll need to practice. It can be tricky at first!

1 Place the thick end of a chopstick in the crook of your thumb.

2 Let the chopstick rest on your ring finger.

3 Place the other chopstick between the tips of your first two fingers and the tip of your thumb.

4 To grab food, move the top chopstick up and down.

Off to School

We go to school, or *hakkyo* (hahk-gyoh), for 12 years. Our school year starts in March and finishes at the end of December. While American kids have their longest vacation in summer, ours is in the winter. Nearly everybody in South Korea can read and write.

During the last year of high school, we take a very difficult test. The test lasts all day. Our scores determine where we go to college. Students study every night for months to prepare for it. Talk about pressure! Most students go to special cram schools every day to prepare. Lessons here last up to five hours. That's on top of our regular school day.

친구
(ching-gu)
friend

One of the main things we learn in school is how to read and write Korean. Our alphabet is called *Hangŭl* (huhn-gul). It is based on Chinese characters that were developed in the 1400s. Each character is based on the shape of your mouth, throat, or tongue when you say the sound. We also learn English in school, and most people here can speak it.

In South Korea, we have two types of numbers. We use them for different things. Sino-Korean numbers come from Chinese numbers. They are used for things like dates, money, measurements, addresses, phone numbers, minutes, and seconds. Native Korean numbers are used for counting objects or people, hours, age, and other things.

Here's how you count to 10 with native Korean numbers. Pay attention to how the numbers are written.

1	하나	hana *(hah-nah)*
2	둘	tul *(dhool)*
3	셋	set *(seht)*
4	넷	net *(neht)*
5	다섯	tasŏt *(dho-sot)*
6	여섯	yŏsŏt *(yo-sot)*
7	일곱	ilgop *(eel-gope)*
8	여덟	yŏdŏl *(yo-dol)*
9	아홉	ahop *(ah-hope)*
10	열	yŏl *(yol)*

Korean Proverbs

In school, we learn a lot of **proverbs**. These sayings give advice and teach truths about life.

Proverb: Even monkeys fall from trees.

Meaning: No one is perfect. Even experts make mistakes.

Proverb: Plant a soybean and a soybean grows. Plant a red bean and a red bean grows.

Meaning: You get out what you put in. Study hard for a test and the test will be easier for you. It can also be said about families. Children tend to be like the people who raise them.

Proverb: If you want to catch a tiger, you have to go to the tiger's cave.

Meaning: You must work hard and take on challenges to achieve your goals.

Proverb: At the end of hardship comes happiness.

Meaning: Never give up. Hard work ends in success, so keep trying.

Proverb: Don't drink the kimchi soup first.

Meaning: Don't get ahead of yourself. Take your time, plan things carefully, and do them in the right order.

Proverb: Birds listen to day words, and rats listen to night words.

Meaning: Be careful what you say and where you say it. People might overhear your words, so speak kindly.

Proverb: It is spilled water.

Meaning: Don't worry about small, minor things. They don't really matter in the long run.

13

Han River in Seoul

Namdaemun Market

Touring South Korea

Seoul: Capital City

Welcome to our city, Seoul. It's the capital and largest city in South Korea. It sits on the banks of the Han River. People have lived in our city for more than 2,000 years. If you visit, the first thing you'll want to do is go to the N Seoul Tower. It's on the top of Mount Nam. Visitors there have an amazing view of the city. In and around the base building, there's a lot to see and do, too.

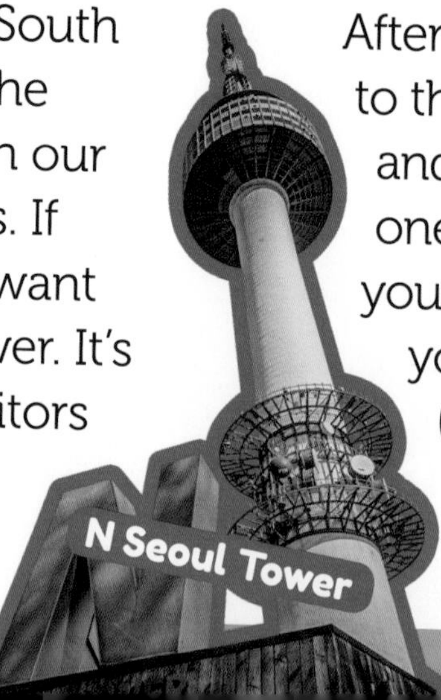

After that, you can head over to the Namdaemun Market and shop till you drop. It's one of many city markets. If you're ever there, make sure you are ready for *enuri* (eh-noo-ree), or haggling. That's the only way to get a good deal.

N Seoul Tower

Gyeongbokgung Palace

Incheon

Next, stop by the beautiful Gyeongbokgung Palace. It was built about 700 years ago for a ruler in the Chosŏn **dynasty**. A dynasty is a series of rulers who are from the same family. At the palace, there are beautiful buildings, majestic gates, and people dressed in clothing from our country's past. It's like stepping back in time.

Jayu Park

Nearby is the city of Incheon. That's where our big airport is located. Like Seoul, Incheon is a busy harbor on the Han River. People can take a stroll through the Jayu (or Freedom) Park. A statue of U.S. general Douglas MacArthur stands there. South Korea and the United States have been friends for a long time!

Busan beach

Daegu Fashion Fair

Busan and Daegu

Because more than 80 percent of people live in cities here, there are many cities to see. Busan is called our summer capital. I love the beaches there. It is our second-largest city and a busy port, too. The popular fish market Jagalchi is there. You'd be amazed at the variety of sea creatures for sale.

Daegu is our fashion city. Each year, we have a big Fashion Fair. My little sister loves seeing all the new clothes. She wants to be a fashion designer one day. People come from all over the world to see these designs. They also come to see the giant stone statue of Buddha, the founder of Buddhism. This statue is called Gatbawi. It is unique because it is wearing a traditional Korean hat, or *gat*. Few Buddha statues have one.

Gatbawi Buddha

Musk deer

Dadohaehaesang National Park

Outdoor Adventure

If you ever come to South Korea, you must visit one of our national parks. My family's favorite is the Seoraksan National Park in northeastern South Korea. Many rare plants and animals live there. These include the Korean goral, musk deer, and edelweiss plant.

Edelweiss

The Dadohaehaesang National Park is South Korea's largest national park. It is home to miles of coastline, beautiful evergreen forests, and many islands. Volcanic activity from the past has created quite a few interesting rock formations, too. If you visit one day, be sure to bring your camera!

Our Country's History

People have lived on this peninsula for about 6,000 years. At times, other countries controlled parts of our land. These included China, Mongolia, and Japan. In the 1500s, Korea fought back by closing its borders. We became known as the "**Hermit** Kingdom."

That ended in the 1850s. Japan and China invaded, and Japan took control in 1910. Then Japan lost World War II (1939–1945). Korea was split between two of the war's winners. The United States controlled the south, which developed a **democratic** government.

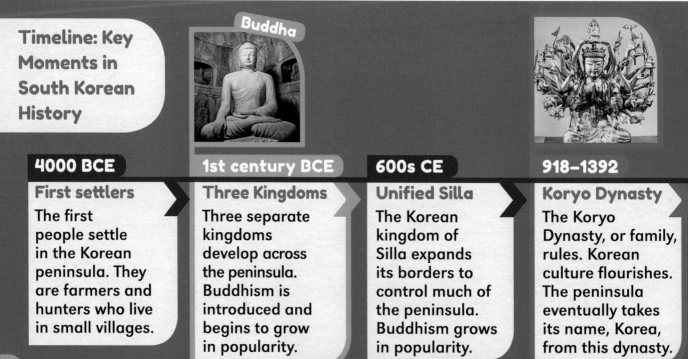

Timeline: Key Moments in South Korean History

Buddha

4000 BCE

First settlers

The first people settle in the Korean peninsula. They are farmers and hunters who live in small villages.

1st century BCE

Three Kingdoms

Three separate kingdoms develop across the peninsula. Buddhism is introduced and begins to grow in popularity.

600s CE

Unified Silla

The Korean kingdom of Silla expands its borders to control much of the peninsula. Buddhism grows in popularity.

918–1392

Koryo Dynasty

The Koryo Dynasty, or family, rules. Korean culture flourishes. The peninsula eventually takes its name, Korea, from this dynasty.

The Soviet Union (now Russia) controlled the north. North Korea had a **communist** government. A single group controlled the government and the economy. North and South were supposed to eventually reunite, but that never happened. North and South Korea fought a bitter war for control. Neither side won, and we remain apart.

The two countries do not always get along. But in 2018, our countries' leaders began to talk about new agreements for peace.

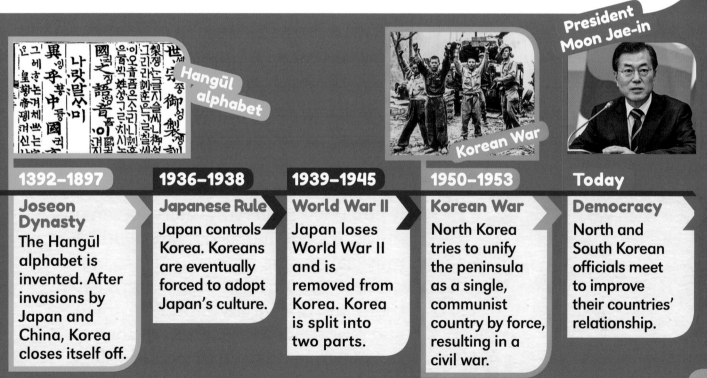

Hangūl alphabet

President Moon Jae-in

Korean War

1392–1897	1936–1938	1939–1945	1950–1953	Today
Joseon Dynasty The Hangūl alphabet is invented. After invasions by Japan and China, Korea closes itself off.	**Japanese Rule** Japan controls Korea. Koreans are eventually forced to adopt Japan's culture.	**World War II** Japan loses World War II and is removed from Korea. Korea is split into two parts.	**Korean War** North Korea tries to unify the peninsula as a single, communist country by force, resulting in a civil war.	**Democracy** North and South Korean officials meet to improve their countries' relationship.

19

It Came From South Korea

Bojagi **are colorful square cloths.** They can be spotted everywhere. They are used to wrap things. You can also store or carry things in them.

We have many special animals. The Amur tiger often appears in South Korean myths and folktales. It is one of our most important national **symbols**. Unfortunately, no one has seen this tiger in the wild for a long time.

Have you heard the fresh sounds of K-pop? K-pop is what everyone calls Korean pop music. It's popular all over the world. K-pop musicians range from solo acts to big groups. The music is known for its catchy tunes and upbeat rhythms. Performances and music videos are often dazzling with stylish outfits and cool dance steps.

Calligraphy is popular in our country. It is a form of fancy, artistic writing. We practice it in school.

We use four tools in calligraphy. They are called "the scholar's four friends." These include the brush, paper, ink stick, and ink stone. We make our own ink by adding water to the ink stone and rubbing the ink stick against it. It's very relaxing.

Masks have a long history in South Korea. People have used them in religious ceremonies for centuries. Long ago, farmers also used them to take a break from their work and have a little fun. There are even plays that use dancing and masks. They are super fun. The audience joins in—clapping, laughing, and sometimes dancing. Here are two common masks.

Nobleman: Sometimes, this mask can do something really strange. When the actor looks up, the mask looks happy. When the actor looks down, the mask looks mean. You have to see it to believe it!

Old Granny: In masked shows, the actor wearing this mask is often gossiping! This mask is my sister's favorite.

Make a Korean Kite

Celebrate!

Everyone loves a holiday, and we have some fun ones in South Korea. My favorite is on May 5. It's Children's Day, or Eorininal. Children's author Pang Chong-hwan invented this holiday. Schools close, and families spend the day together. We have parades and festivals. Visits to museums or amusement parks are free! We get gifts from our parents, too. Some local stores also hand out small gifts. It's our special day!

Long ago, kite battles were popular. The kite string was covered in bits of glass. The goal was to use the string of your kite to cut the kite string of an opponent. Slash! Off flew their kite. Today, we fly kites on important holidays.

What you'll need:
cup about 3 inches wide, sheet of paper, sharp pencil, scissors, five 12-inch straight and narrow sticks (such as bamboo), clear tape, two or three 30-inch lengths of crepe paper, three 2-foot pieces of yarn

1 Use the cup to trace and cut out a circle from the middle of the paper. Set the circle aside. On the paper, draw a design on one side. This will be the front of your kite.

2 Put one bamboo stick across a short edge of the blank side of the paper. This will be your kite's top edge. Roll the paper around the stick once and tape in place.

3 Put a piece of tape on each top corner of the kite, just below the stick. Poke a small hole through these taped spots with your pencil.

4 Put two sticks across the back, from corner to corner, in an X. Place the last stick down the center, from top to bottom. Trim the sticks if they go beyond the kite's edges. Tape them in place.

5 Tape crepe paper tails to the bottom of the kite.

6 Thread a piece of yarn through each of the two small holes you made in step 3. Wrap it around the top stick and tie it tightly. Tie a third piece of yarn to the sticks where they cross in the kite's center hole. Tie the yarn pieces together in a knot about 20 inches from the kite.

Other Fun Celebrations

January February

Seol-nal (Lunar New Year)
We dress in old-style clothes called *hanbok*. After a thorough housecleaning, families eat together. Kids get money in colorful envelopes. We also fly kites or play games like *jegi*.

July

Mud Festival
This is held in Boryeong each year, and people enjoy many mud-filled activities. It's messy fun at its best!

September October

Chuseok (Harvest Moon Festival)
This harvest festival lasts for three days during a full moon. No one works, and there's no school! We clean our **ancestors**' graves. We also play games and eat a special meal with our family.

October

Dangun Day (National Foundation Day)
This holiday celebrates Dangun, the legendary ancient leader and founder of Korea.

23

A woman sleds down an ice slope.

Tae kwon do

Ssireum wrestling

Time to Play

Jump! Spin! Kick! We love sports. *Tae kwon do* is a favorite. This ancient martial art of self-defense started here. Its name means "the way of the foot and fist." High, spinning kicks are popular moves. Experts at the sport can break a wood plank with one kick or punch. Whoa! Someday Yu-na will be able to do that. She looks forward to her tae kwon do class all week.

Winter sports are also big here. We even hosted the 2018 Winter Olympics! We have great, snowy mountains that are perfect for snowboarding, sledding, and skiing.

The oldest sport in our country is a form of wrestling called *ssireum*. Wrestlers battle in a ring. The winner is the wrestler who forces an opponent to touch the ground with any part of his or her body above the knee.

Baduk

We also like to play board games such as *Baduk*. It is a fun game of strategy. Another game we play together at home is *gonggi*. It looks like jacks, except it has no ball.

Korean seesaw, called *neolttwigi*, is something special. Instead of sitting, we stand and jump. The goal is to bounce higher and higher! Some people say it started long ago when girls weren't allowed to leave their fenced-in yards. They played neolttwigi to catch glimpses over the fence. Today, we all play it—at least, those who are brave enough!

You Won't Believe This!

In many countries, a baby celebrates his or her first birthday one year after being born. But not in Korea. A baby is considered to be a one-year-old on the day he or she is born.

When someone turns 60 years old, it is a special and honored event. We have a big party called a *hwangap*. We eat, listen to music, sing, read poetry, and more. Then we take a big family picture.

You might see people in Korea wearing surgical masks. Don't be alarmed. We are very careful not to spread germs. No sneezing or coughing at or near people in public. Masks help us keep those around us safe and healthy.

South Korea is one of the most connected countries in the world. You can access the internet from anywhere!

About half of all Koreans do not have apocrine glands. These are the glands that produce body odor when you sweat. Jealous?

Bowing is very important in South Korea. It is how we show respect to others. It comes from a set of beliefs known as Confucianism. The higher someone's status is, the lower a person bows to them. We also bow when we say "please" and "thank you." We even bow to get someone's attention in a store.

The crane is a symbol of good luck for us. Red-crowned cranes are found in South Korea. At about 5 feet (1.5 meters) tall, they are quite large for a bird. Magpies, called *kkachi*, are also very popular birds. Many cities in Korea have made this chatty animal their official bird. People say its constant chattering represents the hopeful spirit of Korea's people.

How to Bow

1 Stand straight. Make eye contact.

2 Bend forward at the waist and look down. Keep your hands at your sides or hold them in front of you.

3 Say something, such as "thank you." Straighten up and make eye contact.

Guessing Game!

Here are some other great sites around South Korea. If you have time, try to see them all!

1 Bomun Lake
2 Gosu Cave
3 Mount Halla
4 Myeongdong Cathedral
5 Korean Folk Village
6 Ulleungdo Island
7 Manggyeongsa Temple

Cool-looking stalactites and stalagmites fill this limestone cave. But be on the lookout for the bats!

E

A

This village is full of traditional buildings, activities, and food. It is in the city of Yongin.

This human-made lake is a popular tourist spot.

B

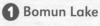

F

Our tallest mountain, located on Jeju Island, is also a volcano.

This temple in the Taebaek Mountains is a must-see.

G

D

This cathedral, or church, is Seoul's center for Christianity.

C

This island off Korea's eastern coast was formed by a volcano.

Preparing for Your Visit

You might have the chance to see South Korea in person someday. Here are some tips that could help you prepare for a trip.

1 Before you come to South Korea, exchange your money. Our money is called won. It comes in many fun colors. There are pictures of famous South Korean people and buildings on it, too. One woman, Shin Saimdang, is shown. She is famous for being a poet, artist, and wise mother.

2 Summer in South Korea is hot and humid. Winter is cold and snowy. Spring and fall have mild, comfortable temperatures. Keep this in mind as you pack.

3 Our street addresses work differently from those in the United States. Cities here are divided into wards (*gu*). Wards are divided into districts, and districts are made up of smaller sections or blocks (*ka*). An address in Seoul might be: Seoul (city), Gangnum-gu (ward), Cheongdam-dong (district), #7 (building number on the block). Building numbers are where it can get confusing. Buildings are numbered based on the order in which they were built, not where they are in the block. If traveling from a hotel, ask the person at the front desk for an address card. You can give the card to a taxi driver or ask someone for help.

4 Friendship is very important to us. Smile, bow, and learn a few Korean words before you visit. You're bound to make friends.

5 South Korea has a great public transportation. It's fast and affordable. Plus, the same card works for public trains and buses in several cities.

The United States Compared to South Korea

	United States of America (USA)	Republic of Korea
Official Name	United States of America (USA)	Republic of Korea
Official Language	No official language, though English is most commonly used	Korean
Population	325 million	Over 48 million
Common Words	yes, no, please, thank you	ne (neh), aniyo (ah-nee-yoh), juseyo (joo-seh-yoh), gamsa hamnida (gahm-sah ham-nee-dah)
Flag		
Money	Dollar	Won
Location	North America	East Asia
Highest Point	Denali (Mount McKinley)	Mount Halla
Lowest Point	Death Valley	Sea level along the coast
National Anthem	"The Star-Spangled Banner"	"Aegukka" ("The Patriotic Song" or "Love the Country")

So now you know some important and fascinating things about our country, South Korea. We hope to see you someday touring one of our bustling cities, snowboarding on one of our mountains, or enjoying a bowl of kimchi. Until then . . . *annyonghi kyeseyo* (ahn-nyohng-hee kuh-say-yoh)! Good-bye!

Glossary

ancestors
(AN-ses-turz)
members of a family who lived long ago

calligraphy
(kuh-LIG-ruh-fee)
decorative handwriting

communist
(KAH-myoo-nist)
of or having to do with organizing the economy of a country so that all the land, property, businesses, and resources belong to the government or community, and the profits are shared by all

democratic
(dem-uh-KRAT-ik)
of or having to do with a form of government in which people choose their leaders in elections

dynasty
(DYE-nuh-stee)
a series of rulers belonging to the same family

hermit
(HUR-mit)
living alone and staying away from other people

peninsula
(puh-NIN-suh-luh)
a piece of land that sticks out from a larger landmass and is almost completely surrounded by water

proverbs
(PRAH-vurbz)
familiar sayings that tell a common truth

symbols
(SIM-buhlz)
designs or objects that stand for, suggest, or represent something else

Index

Facts for Now

Visit this Scholastic website for more information on South Korea and to download the Teaching Guide for this series:

www.factsfornow.scholastic.com   Enter the keywords **South Korea**

About the Author

Wiley Blevins is from New York City. His greatest love is traveling, and he has been all over the world, including

Korea. In addition to Follow Me Around books, he has written the Ick and Crud series and the Scary Tales Retold series.